CONNECT BIBLE STUDIES

Iris

Dir. Richard Eyre
(Buena Vista, 2001)

Living
Communicating
Caring
Dying

www.connectbiblestudies.com

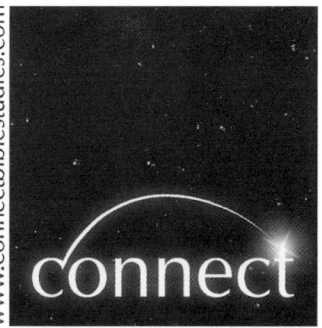

connect

linking the Word to the world

CONNECT BIBLE STUDIES: Iris

Published in this format by Scripture Union, 207-209 Queensway, Bletchley, MK2 2EB, England.

Scripture Union is an international Christian charity working with churches in more than 130 countries providing resources to bring the good news about Jesus Christ to children, young people and families — and to encourage them to develop spiritually through the Bible and prayer.

As well as a network of volunteers, staff and associates who run holidays, church-based events and school Christian groups, Scripture Union produces a wide range of publications and supports those who use the resources through training programmes.

Email: info@scriptureunion.org.uk   Internet: www.scriptureunion.org.uk

© Damaris Trust, PO Box 200, Southampton, SO17 2DL.

Damaris Trust enables people to relate Christian faith and contemporary culture. It helps them to think about the issues within society from a Christian perspective and to explore God's truth as it is revealed in the Bible. Damaris provides resources via the Internet, workshops, publications and products.

Email: office@damaris.org   Internet: www.damaris.org

ALSO AVAILABLE AS AN ELECTRONIC DOWNLOAD: www.connectbiblestudies.com

Chief editor: Nick Pollard
Consultant Editor: Andrew Clark
Managing Editor: Di Archer
Written by Di Archer, James Murkett, Caroline Puntis, Tony Watkins

First published 2002
ISBN 1 85999 669 8

British Library Cataloguing-in-Publication Data: a catalogue record for this book is available from the British Library.

Cover design and print production by:
CPO, Garcia Estate, Canterbury Road, Worthing, West Sussex BN13 1BW.

Other titles in this series:

Harry Potter and the Goblet of Fire ISBN 1 85999 578 0
The Matrix ISBN 1 85999 579 9
U2: All that you can't leave behind ISBN 1 85999 580 2
Billy Elliot ISBN 1 85999 581 0
Chocolat ISBN 1 85999 608 6
Game Shows ISBN 1 85999 609 4
How to be Good ISBN 1 85999 610 8
Destiny's Child: Survivor ISBN 1 85999 613 2
AI (Artificial Intelligence) ISBN 1 85999 626 4
The Lord of the Rings ISBN 1 85999 634 5
The Simpsons ISBN 1 85999 529 2

And more titles following — check www.connectbiblestudies.com for latest titles or ask at any good Christian bookshop.

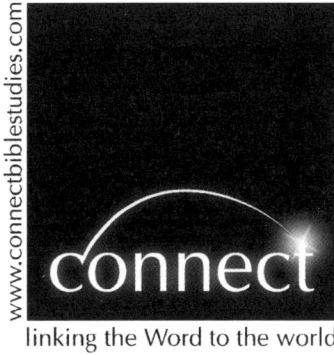

Using Connect Bible Studies

connect

linking the Word to the world

What Are These Studies?

These innovative home group Bible studies have two aims. Firstly, we design them to enable group members to dig into their Bibles and get to know them better. Secondly, we aim to help members to think through topical issues in a Biblical way. Hence the studies are based on a current popular book or film etc. The issues raised by these are the subjects for the Bible studies.

We do not envisage that all members will always be able to watch the films or read the books, or indeed that they will always want to. A summary is always provided. However, our vision is that knowing about these films and books empowers Christians to engage with friends and colleagues about them. Addressing issues from a Biblical perspective gives Christians confidence that they know what they think, and can bring a distinctive angle to bear in conversations.

The studies are produced in sets of four — i.e. four weeks' worth of group Bible Study material. These are available in print published by Scripture Union from your local Christian bookshop, or via the Internet at www.connectbiblestudies.com. Anyone can sign up for a free monthly email newsletter that announces the new studies and provides other information (sign up on the Connect Bible Studies website at www.connectbiblestudies.com/uk/register).

How Do I Use Them?

We design the studies to stimulate creative thought and discussion within a Biblical context. Each section therefore has a range of questions or options from which you as leader may choose in order to tailor the study to your group's needs and desires. Different approaches may appeal at different times, so the studies aim to supply lots of choice. Whilst adhering to the main aim of corporate Bible study, some types of questions may enable this for your group better than others — so take your pick.

Group members should be supplied with the appropriate sheet that they can fill in, each one also showing the relevant summary.

Leader's notes contain:

1. Opening Questions

These help your group settle in to discussion, whilst introducing the topics. They may be straightforward, personal or creative, but are aiming to provoke a response.

2. Summary

We suggest the summary of the book or film will follow now, read aloud if necessary. There may well be reactions that group members want to express even before getting on to the week's issue.

3. Key Issue

Again, either read from the leader's notes, or summarised.

4. Bible Study

Lots of choice here. Choose as appropriate to suit your group — get digging into the Bible. Background reading and texts for further help and study are suggested, but please use the material provided to inspire your group to explore their Bibles as much as possible. A concordance might be a handy standby for looking things up. A commentary could be useful too, such as the *New Bible Commentary 21st Century Edition* (IVP, 1994). The idea is to help people to engage with the truth of God's word, wrestling with it if necessary but making it their own.

Don't plan to work through every question here. Within each section the two questions explore roughly the same ground but from different angles or in different ways. Our advice is to take one question from each section. The questions are open-ended so each ought to yield good discussion — though of course any discussion in a Bible study may need prompting to go a little further.

5. Implications

Here the aim is to tie together the perspectives gained through Bible study and the impact of the book or film. The implications may be personal, a change in worldview, or new ideas for relating to non-churchgoers. Choose questions that adapt to the flow of the discussion.

6. Prayer

Leave time for it! We suggest a time of open prayer, or praying in pairs if the group would prefer. Encourage your members to focus on issues from your study that had a particular impact on them. Try different approaches to prayer — light a candle, say a prayer each, write prayers down, play quiet worship music — aim to facilitate everyone to relate to God.

7. Background Reading

You will find links to some background reading on the Connect Bible Studies website: www.connectbiblestudies.com/

8. Online Discussion

You can discuss the studies online with others on the Connect Bible Studies website at www.connectbiblestudies.com/discuss/

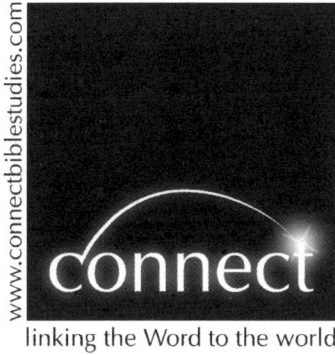

Iris

Dir. Richard Eyre (Buena Vista, 2001)

Part One: Living

'Keep hold of me and it will be all right!'
Young Iris to John, as they cycle down a steep hill

Please read Using Connect Bible Studies *before leading a Bible study using this material.*

Opening Questions

Choose one of these questions.

How did you react to the film 'Iris'?	Does being free mean having no boundaries? Why or why not?
Is education the route to freedom, as Iris said? Why or why not?	Describe someone you know with a real zest for life. How does it show?

Summary

John Bayley first meets Iris Murdoch at an Oxford college dinner in the 1950s. He is captivated by her, as are most of her colleagues — she speaks with wit and authority about everything. Her passions are apparent in all that she says and writes. Her first love is words and she is excited about philosophy and communicating. This isn't just an intellectual exercise — she lives out her ideas.

Iris is determined to experience life to the full. She clearly embraces her sexuality and has had a string of lovers — including women. When John asks her what her first novel is about, she replies, 'How to be free ... how to be good ... and how to love.' John is nonetheless confused by the way she chooses to live her life — how can she ever love him if she is entangled with others in a sexual way?

For some time, their relationship exists as a simple friendship although John is obviously in love with her. Iris believes in exercising her freedom — perhaps not understanding the full cost to the man with whom she will eventually spend the rest of her life.

Key Issue: Living

One thing that shines out from the portrayal of the young Iris in the film is her zest for life. Swimming, cycling, studying – and, arguably, even her questionable sexual adventures — show an Iris who wants to make the most of living. Iris contends that education is the key to a fulfilled life, for it is through education that we know we are happy. But what does the Bible say about teaching and learning? Iris wants the concept of the divine, but without God. What happens when we stop learning about God? How does God engage with our minds? What is the truth about freedom of mind and what is really most important?

Bible Study

In this study we have taken the principles of Iris' philosophy for living and put them in the context of having a relationship with God. Choose one question from each section.

1. **Teaching and learning — about God**

   'Education may be the means by which we realise we are happy.' (Iris)

   ◆ Read Psalm 78:1–8. What does the Psalmist want the people to learn? Why is it so important?

   ◆ Read 2 Timothy 3:10–17. What does Paul want Timothy to understand? How will it affect his life?

2. **Thinking — with God**

   'You call it a job but it's like music. What you do. You live with the angels, speak their language, the music of the spheres.' (John)

   ◆ Read Haggai 1:1–15. What method does God use to show the people the error of their ways? How do the people change?

   Leaders: see also Deuteronomy 28:15–24, 38–42.

   ◆ Read 2 Peter 3:1–13; Philippians 4:8, 9. Why do Peter and Paul commend 'wholesome thinking'? What kinds of things should we think about?

3.   Being free — because of God

'Education ... convinces us that there is only one freedom of any importance whatsoever, that of the mind, and gives us the assurance ... the confidence to walk the path our mind, our educated mind, offers.' (Iris)

◆   Read Exodus 13:11–18; 14:5–31. What is freedom? Is freedom easy? Why?

Leaders: The Israelites' departure from Egypt followed the first Passover (see Exodus 12:1–16) — it was the key moment in their history as a nation. Jesus understood the Passover and Exodus to be a foreshadowing of his sacrificial death and the freedom that comes to the believer who trusts in him.

◆   Read Galatians 5:1–15. For what purpose has Christ set us free? What is Paul so angry about?

Leaders: Paul taught the gospel of grace, not of works. It seems that outsiders had come into the church at Galatia and were teaching that believers also needed to keep the Old Testament law — including circumcision — to be truly saved. Paul fiercely disputed this.

4.   Understanding — in God

'Nothing matters except loving what is good.' (Young Iris)

◆   Read Psalm 119:33–40, 97–104. What did the Psalmist value about God's laws? How did he think they related to himself?

Leaders: A right understanding of Old Testament law does not contradict salvation by grace. The law drives us to Jesus for forgiveness as we see our inability to keep it. Nonetheless, the law still shows us how to live in a way that pleases God in response to his grace.

◆   Read Titus 3:1–15. What is Paul asking Titus to do? How will the people's understanding of God affect their lives?

Implications

'We need to believe in something divine without the need for God, something which we might call Love or Goodness.' (Iris)

Choose one or more of the following questions.

- Iris wanted 'something divine', but without God. How would you answer a friend who sees Christianity as restricting rather than freeing?

- How do we win the battle in our heads and think the way God wants us to?

- What does it mean to you to be free in Christ? How could you explore it more?

- How can we use our freedom to serve one another in love?

- Are there issues or concepts in the Bible that you find difficult? How can you find help to wrestle with them?

- How can you increase your understanding of God?

- How can you have more of a zest for life?

Prayer

Spend some time praying through these issues.

Background Reading

You will find links to some background reading on the Connect Bible Studies website: www.connectbiblestudies.com/uk/catalogue/0012/background.htm

Discuss

Discuss this study in the online discussion forums at www.connectbiblestudies.com/discuss

Members' Sheet: Iris — Part 1

Summary

John Bayley first meets Iris Murdoch at an Oxford college dinner in the 1950s. He is captivated by her, as are most of her colleagues — she speaks with wit and authority about everything. Her passions are apparent in all that she says and writes. Her first love is words and she is excited about philosophy and communicating. This isn't just an intellectual exercise — she lives out her ideas.

Iris is determined to experience life to the full. She clearly embraces her sexuality and has had a string of lovers — including women. When John asks her what her first novel is about, she replies, 'How to be free ... how to be good ... and how to love.' John is nonetheless confused by the way she chooses to live her life — how can she ever love him if she is entangled with others in a sexual way?

For some time, their relationship exists as a simple friendship although John is obviously in love with her. Iris believes in exercising her freedom — perhaps not understanding the full cost to the man with whom she will eventually spend the rest of her life.

Key Issue

Bible Study notes

Implications

Prayer

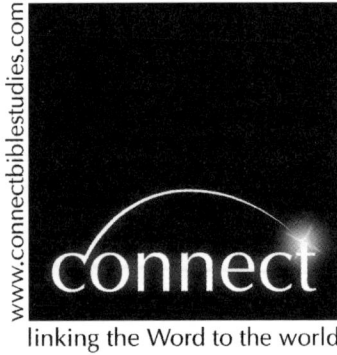

connect

linking the Word to the world

Iris

Dir. Richard Eyre (Buena Vista, 2001)

Part Two: Communicating

'Human beings love each other, in sex, in friendship — and when they are in love. And they cherish other beings, humans, animals, plants, even stones. The quest for happiness is in all of this, and the power of our imagination.'
Iris

Please read Using Connect Bible Studies *before leading a Bible study using this material.*

Opening Questions

Choose one of these questions.

Have you read any of Iris' books? What did you think of them?	Are you a 'huggy' person? Why or why not?
What is your favourite means of communication (eg speaking face to face, writing, on the telephone, etc.)?	How have you expressed love to someone today? How would you like someone to express love to you?

Summary

As a writer, Iris Murdoch lives much of her life in the secret world of her mind. 'It's like living in a fairy story,' says her husband John as a young man. 'I'm ... in love with a beautiful maiden who disappears into an unknown and mysterious world every now and again but who always comes back.' Iris herself values words enormously. Without them, she would be unable to think and unable to create her work.

When John asks her if she sleeps with women, a look is all that he receives in reply. They begin to communicate on many levels as their relationship grows and deepens. Iris gradually lets John into her world, whilst she consumes his upon first sight.

As Alzheimer's disease sets in, Iris progressively loses the ability to communicate with words and John discovers new ways to reach her. Touch becomes vital as Iris grows more and more like a child, tugging at his sleeve and desperately clinging to him in moments of panic.

Key Issue: Communicating

When Alzheimer's disease stole Iris' superb ability to communicate, the tragedy was felt not only by her, but also by her husband John, who desperately tried to help her to carry on writing. Clearly, as a writer, thinker and speaker, Iris set great store by communication. Yet Iris herself had acknowledged other avenues by which we can communicate with each other, apart from words, and these were not entirely lost to her during her illness. We tend to think of the Bible as a long book of words, but how does it communicate to us? Does it deal in pictures too? What does it say about the languages of touch and love which Iris highlighted?

Bible Study

Choose one question from each section.

1. The language of words

'I find it hard to believe that what Iris is saying is of no consequence; her words are her writing, she is making social statements, they are her last remarks before the lights go out.' (John)

♦   Read Proverbs 10:19; 12:25; 15:1; 16:24; 25:11. What power do words have? How and why do they have such power?

♦   Read Matthew 12:33–37. How important are our words and why? What do they really communicate?

2. The language of pictures

'Nowadays the only language everyone really understands is pictures. Paint the picture.' (John)

♦   Read Ezekiel 4:1–17. What would a passing Israelite have seen when he looked at Ezekiel? What did Ezekiel's visual aid communicate?

Leaders: This incident occurred in 593 BC — twelve years after the first group of exiles were taken to Babylon. It seems that those in exile failed to realise that this was more than just a temporary setback for Judah. Ezekiel's task was to make clear to his fellow exiles that much worse was to come back home in Jerusalem because their spiritual state was far more serious than they realised.

♦ Read Mark 4:1–20. How did Jesus use the example of the sower to draw pictures in his hearers' minds? How did he expect them to respond?

Leaders: The response to this parable illustrates the point Jesus is making about parables. It seems parables have the purpose of revealing people's spiritual receptiveness. Those, like the disciples, who ask for more explanation are given it. Whilst others are unreceptive (v 12), they do not truly understand and are judged for this stubbornness.

3. The language of love

'Love, that's the only language that everyone understands.' (Iris)

♦ Read Song of Songs 2:1–7. What does the Lover communicate to the Beloved? How does it affect her?

♦ Read Luke 10:25–37. How does love communicate? How do the Old Testament law, eternal life and love relate to each other?

4. The language of touch

'When we really *speak the truth, words are insufficient.'* (Young Iris)

♦ Read Song of Songs 7:1–13. What descriptions of the Beloved show the Lover thinks she is good to touch? Why does their touching communicate love?

♦ Read Mark 1:40–45. How did Jesus touching the leper communicate love to him? What effect did it have on the man and on Jesus?

Leaders: The man with the infectious skin disease was ceremonially unclean — hence the instruction to offer sacrifices upon his healing. He would have been an outcast and excluded from Jewish society. For Jesus to touch the man initially and to restore him to health as well was good news.

Implications

'Love, yes, I can read it but I can't speak it.' (John)

Choose one or more of the following questions.

♦   Words can hurt or heal. Is there forgiveness you must offer for harsh words said to you? Or apologies to make? How can our words be a force for good?

♦   What is love? How do you communicate this to different types of people?

♦   Jesus did not hesitate to touch a leper. How can we use touch appropriately to bring healing to others?

♦   Are there rights and wrongs about the use of touch within a Christian community? What about outside it?

♦   If you are artistic, how can you use your talent and enthusiasm to communicate our faith?

♦   How much value do you put on communicating with others in different ways? How could you improve your communication?

♦   How are these different forms of communication important — especially within marriage? Which aspects do you need to work on?

♦   What would you say to someone who agrees with Iris that communication between humans takes the various forms of words, pictures, love and touch but doesn't think this has anything to do with God?

Prayer

Spend some time praying through these issues.

Background Reading

You will find links to some background reading on the Connect Bible Studies website: www.connectbiblestudies.com/uk/catalogue/0012/background.htm

Discuss

Discuss this study in the online discussion forums at www.connectbiblestudies.com/discuss

Members' Sheet: Iris — Part 2

Summary

As a writer, Iris Murdoch lives much of her life in the secret world of her mind. 'It's like living in a fairy story,' says her husband John as a young man. 'I'm ... in love with a beautiful maiden who disappears into an unknown and mysterious world every now and again but who always comes back.' Iris herself values words enormously. Without them, she would be unable to think and unable to create her work.

When John asks her if she sleeps with women, a look is all that he receives in reply. They begin to communicate on many levels as their relationship grows and deepens. Iris gradually lets John into her world, whilst she consumes his upon first sight.

As Alzheimer's disease sets in, Iris progressively loses the ability to communicate with words and John discovers new ways to reach her. Touch becomes vital as Iris grows more and more like a child, tugging at his sleeve and desperately clinging to him in moments of panic.

Key Issue

Bible Study notes

Implications

Prayer

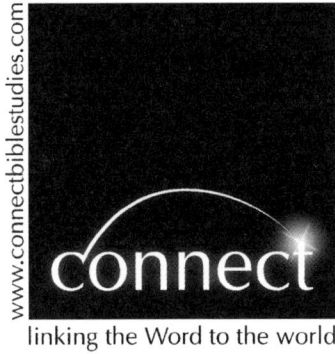

Iris

Dir. Richard Eyre (Buena Vista, 2001)

Part Three: Caring

'We'll get ourselves home and then there'll be tomorrow and the next day and the next ... and on we go growing closer and closest together.'
John

Please read Using Connect Bible Studies *before leading a Bible study using this material.*

Opening Questions

Choose one of these questions.

What do you think of the way John cared for Iris in the film?	Why is change so often stressful?
How would you define the role of a 'carer'?	How do you appreciate being cared for?

Summary

When Iris' illness prevails, it soon becomes clear that her husband John has never had to care for anyone before — including himself. Iris used to do everything; now she can do nothing. John does his best to look after her, but he has little experience to draw upon when it comes to the basics of cooking and cleaning. Their doctor offers him help several times, but John refuses, believing that he and Iris are too odd to receive aid from strangers.

Part of John's struggle is in accepting that Iris will never recover. She is very difficult to live with and his emotional journey is incredibly harrowing — he moves from anger and frustration to pity and sorrow in mere moments. Sometimes he even hates her. As they lie in bed one night, John is haunted by memories of the past. When they were young, John felt that Iris belonged to other lovers — now they have moved out of her life and he has her, but no longer wants her.

Eventually John is forced to let her go. He can no longer cope on his own and Iris needs professional care. Reluctantly, he takes her to a nursing home, where she dies quietly and peacefully.

Key Issue: Caring

As Iris slowly loses her mind to Alzheimer's disease, her husband John is forced into the position of carer. His devotion to Iris is unquestionable, but he struggles with the implications of her degenerating health. His distress is evident as he tries to care for her, while coping with her mood swings and unpredictable behaviour. Thus disease forces John into a role he would not have chosen. Many of us can identify with John's predicament to one extent or another. When others are dependent on us, where can we turn to in the Bible to find comfort? Can the Bible help us with the grief and adjustment that often accompanies unwelcome change? How does the carer get cared for?

Bible Study

Choose one question from each section.

1. Facing loss

'It was so quiet. When she died. Do you know, I thought: I wouldn't mind doing that myself ... I had a joke to tell her, not ... no, not a very good one but she would've laughed.' (John)

♦ Read 2 Samuel 1:1–27. Describe David's feelings at the death of Saul and Jonathan. How did death change David's world?

Leaders: Bear in mind that David could have been expected to rejoice over Saul's death — after all, Saul had tried to kill him on several occasions.

♦ Read John 11:1–44. How did Jesus initially react to the death of his friend? Why did death not have the last word?

2. Taking care of people

'Please don't, Iris, you have no reason to be sorry for anything, it wouldn't be fair and I couldn't bear it. We have to say sorry to you ...' (John)

♦ Read 2 Samuel 9:1–13. What was David's motivation in caring for Mephibosheth? To what extent did the King ensure that Mephibosheth's needs were met?

- Read Matthew 25:31–46. 'These brothers of mine' (v. 40) refers to all Jesus' followers. What is the big surprise for the people to whom Jesus is speaking? What do our actions reveal about our relationship with Jesus?

    Leaders: This passage is often taken to mean that people are judged on how they care for others — especially for disadvantaged people. But v. 40 makes clear that Jesus is talking about how all people treat his followers (see also Matthew 12:48, 49; 28:10). It is an outward evidence of how they have responded to Jesus.

3.   Making changes

She does everything, always has — where we go ... food ... shopping ... tickets for things. I'm impossible about such things. I never know how she manages and does her books as well, order fuel and pay people ...' (John)

- Read Ruth 1:1–22. What were the consequences of the women's bereavements? What changes was Ruth prepared to make in order to care for her bereaved mother-in-law?

- Read Luke 2:34,35 and John 19:25-27. What changes does Simeon anticipate that Jesus will bring to Mary? What are the implications of Jesus' words to Mary and John?

4.   Being comforted

Dr Gudgeon: ***There is always help if you need it.***
John: ***There isn't any for her.***

- Read Isaiah 49:8–26. How will God comfort Israel? In what ways do these promises have a wider application?

    Leaders: This passage is one of several that promise restoration for Israel after a time of judgment. These promises were fulfilled when the people returned to Judah after the exile — but only partially. It was not a return to the golden age of the reigns of David and Solomon. As a result, God's people began to realise that there is a fuller fulfilment of these promises still to come when God establishes the new heavens and the new earth.

- Read 2 Corinthians 1:3–7; 7:5–7. What comfort does God offer? How does it work? What are the consequences?

Implications

'I used to be afraid of being alone with you, and now I can't be without you.' (John)

Choose one or more of the following questions.

♦ What would you say to a friend who argues that Iris' suffering, and that of others like her, proves there is no God?

♦ Do you really trust God to meet your needs and rely on his strength for your daily challenges? How could you do so more?

♦ Is your understanding of God big enough for the hard times? If not, how could it grow?

♦ Enforced change can bring about grief and anger. Can you express all your emotions to God, whatever they are? If not, what can you do about it?

♦ What are the rewards of caring for others?

♦ What encouragement can you give to long-term carers whom you know?

Prayer

Are there people in your group who are caring for others? Spend some time praying for them especially.

Background Reading

You will find links to some background reading on the Connect Bible Studies website: www.connectbiblestudies.com/uk/catalogue/0012/background.htm

Discuss

Discuss this study in the online discussion forums at www.connectbiblestudies.com/discuss

Members' Sheet: Iris — Part 3

Summary

When Iris' illness prevails, it soon becomes clear that her husband John has never had to care for anyone before — including himself. Iris used to do everything; now she can do nothing. John does his best to look after her, but he has little experience to draw upon when it comes to the basics of cooking and cleaning. Their doctor offers him help several times, but John refuses, believing that he and Iris are too odd to receive aid from strangers.

Part of John's struggle is in accepting that Iris will never recover. She is very difficult to live with and his emotional journey is incredibly harrowing — he moves from anger and frustration to pity and sorrow in mere moments. Sometimes he even hates her. As they lie in bed one night, John is haunted by memories of the past. When they were young, John felt that Iris belonged to other lovers — now they have moved out of her life and he has her, but no longer wants her.

Eventually John is forced to let her go. He can no longer cope on his own and Iris needs professional care. Reluctantly, he takes her to a nursing home, where she dies quietly and peacefully.

Key Issue

Bible Study notes

Implications

Prayer

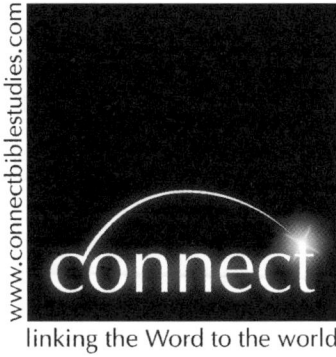

connect

linking the Word to the world

Iris

Dir. Richard Eyre (Buena Vista, 2001)

Part Four: Dying

'I feel as if I'm sailing into darkness.'
Iris

Please read Using Connect Bible Studies *before leading a Bible study using this material.*

Opening Questions

Choose one of these questions.

Is dying the worst thing that can happen to us? Why or why not?	Have you ever been close to dying? What happened?
Why is death such a taboo subject in Western culture?	Do you think that people in general believe in life after death?

Summary

Alzheimer's disease creeps up on Iris almost without her noticing. She begins to repeat herself and sometimes loses words completely. As a prolific writer, words had always been her greatest ally — now they are the enemy. Half way through doing an interview with the BBC she forgets what she is saying and has no idea why she is there. Familiar words lose their meaning, but, she explains, 'I know what the words mean. To me.' Senseless words start to form on her lips and she struggles to say anything that has real meaning to others.

Her inability to communicate effectively, combined with a series of panic attacks, seriously affects her relationships. Firstly, tension grows between Iris and her husband, John. The way that he struggles to care for her is mirrored in her difficulty with being looked after. Iris simply does not have control of her life anymore.

When the day comes to go to the nursing home, Iris resists like a child, unwilling to leave the safety of the stairs. The taxi driver jovially teases her down and they set off on what is to be her final journey.

Key Issue: Dying

Judi Dench's portrayal of the deterioration Iris Murdoch endured is powerful and moving. Alzheimer's disease reduced an intelligent, enthusiastic lover of life to a bewildered dependant. At the beginning of the process, Iris was most frightened of losing her mind. But her body suffered too. So how realistic is the Bible about the challenge of long-term illness? Did Bible characters have a smooth ride, or can they help us face these difficult times? What does the Bible say about the pathway to death? And finally, what does the good news of resurrection really mean?

Bible Study

Choose one question from each section.

1.   Loss of health

'We all worry about going mad, don't we? How would we know, those of us who live in our minds, anyway? Other people would tell us. Would they, John?' (Iris)

♦   Read Psalm 38:1–22. Why was David in dire straights? What effect did his predicament have on his outlook?

♦   Read Isaiah 38:1–22. How did Hezekiah express his initial anguish before God? How did his reprieve affect his relationship with God?

2.   Loss of interaction

'There are some drugs, aren't there, Iris? But they don't last long and when the friendly fog disperses, there yawns the precipice before you ...' (John)

♦   Read Psalm 88:1–18. What impact did the Psalmist's illness have on his relationships? What was the effect on his outlook?

♦   Read Ecclesiastes 11:7–12:8. How does the writer of Ecclesiastes picture the gradual decline in health and interaction? Why does he conclude everything is meaningless?

3. Loss of life

'I hate new things. I like things that are worn down, worn out, which wear and wear and wear ... until they go.' (Young Iris)

♦   Read Ecclesiastes 9:1–12. What does the writer say about our common destiny? What good things could come out of this understanding?

♦   Read 1 Corinthians 15:20–23, 35–55. What does Paul say about why we die? What does he say about living?

Leaders: note that this passage is used again in the next section — you may like your group to look at both questions.

4. Loss of death

'Love, extreme love, once it's recognised, has the stamp of the indubitable.'
(Young Iris)

♦   Read 1 Thessalonians 4:13–18. Why do believers not need to grieve in the same way as those 'who have no hope'? What are we to do with this knowledge?

Leaders: It appears that the Thessalonians had not fully understood the hope of the resurrection of the dead. When Christ returns, he will come with those who 'have fallen asleep in him' (v 14). They will be reunited with those who are still alive. Those 'asleep' in Christ will not miss out on anything.

♦   Read 1 Corinthians 15:20–23, 35–55. What is Paul trying to explain to the Corinthian church? What is the good news about death?

Implications

'I know what it is and it doesn't surprise me, it frightens me, but sometimes it doesn't frighten me and that's just as bad because that's it winning, isn't it? ... It will win.' (Iris talking about her Alzheimer's disease)

Choose one or more of the following questions.

♦ How can we encourage each other when we face long-term suffering?

♦ The Victorians were encouraged to pray for a 'good death'. What would it mean for us to do the same?

♦ How can we support those who are dying?

♦ If our own death is a difficult subject to think or talk about, how can we let God help us, and how can we help each other?

♦ What would you say to someone who argues that there in no point in life because of the inevitability of death?

♦ How does what we know about the new heavens and the new earth help us cope with death and dying?

♦ How would you answer someone who seems quite happy with the conviction that there is no life after death?

Prayer

Is there anyone in your group who is particularly struggling with these issues at present? Spend some time praying specifically for them. Your group might also like to spend some time praying for the members to have an eternal perspective on their lives now that will help them face the prospect of their own death or that of others close to them. You could meditate on some verses from Psalm 90 and Revelation 21:1–7.

Background Reading

You will find links to some background reading on the Connect Bible Studies website: www.connectbiblestudies.com/uk/catalogue/0012/background.htm

Discuss

Discuss this study in the online discussion forums at www.connectbiblestudies.com/discuss

Members' Sheet: Iris — Part 4

Summary

Alzheimer's disease creeps up on Iris almost without her noticing. She begins to repeat herself and sometimes loses words completely. As a prolific writer, words had always been her greatest ally — now they are the enemy. Half way through doing an interview with the BBC she forgets what she is saying and has no idea why she is there. Familiar words lose their meaning, but, she explains, 'I know what the words mean. To me.' Senseless words start to form on her lips and she struggles to say anything that has real meaning to others.

Her inability to communicate effectively, combined with a series of panic attacks, seriously affects her relationships. Firstly, tension grows between Iris and her husband, John. The way that he struggles to care for her is mirrored in her difficulty with being looked after. Iris simply does not have control of her life anymore.

When the day comes to go to the nursing home, Iris resists like a child, unwilling to leave the safety of the stairs. The taxi driver jovially teases her down and they set off on what is to be her final journey.

Key Issue

Bible Study notes

Implications

Prayer